Ben's treasure h

Story by Beverley Randell
Illustrated by Genevieve Rees

Mom said,

"Ben, come here.

Here is a clue for you."

Ben went to look
on the swing.
"A clue!" he shouted.

Ben went to look
on the television.
"A clue!" he shouted.

Clue 3
Look on the
table.

7

Ben went to look
on the table.
"A clue!" he shouted.

Clue 4
Look
on
Teddy
Bear.

Ben went to look
on Teddy Bear.
"A clue!" he shouted.

Clue 5
Look in
Mom's
pocket.

Ben went to look
in Mom's pocket.

"A plane!" shouted Ben.

"I love you, Mom," said Ben.